This Book Belongs to:

_____

To order additional copies of this book, contact:
Xlibris
844-714-8691
www.Xlibris.com
Orders@Xlibris.com

ISBN: Softcover   978-1-4134-1029-7
       Hardcover   978-1-4134-4159-8
       EBook   978-1-6698-6288-8

Library of Congress Control Number: 2003093297

Print information available on the last page

Rev. date: 01/12/2023

Gray

the

Stray

written & illustrated

by

Trudy L. Himes

Gray the Stray

I saw a stray along my way,
All fur and bones and tail.
He looked at me with eyes of gold
And followed while he wailed.

Home we went to find a vet.
He looked so ill and frail.
A pill or two and lots of love
Now finds a wagging tail.

He wears a coat of gray and white,
A tailor made tuxedo.
Not always needing formal wear,
He travels incognito.

His normal bath does not suffice.
He showers with me daily.
Now's the time he gives advice
And sings like Pearl Bailey!

Looking fit for basketball,
His shape betrays his vice.
Having snacks beneath the sun.
Look out you fat, sweet mice!

On my bed he loves to sleep.
For hours he's curled away.
Throughout the night he purrs his thanks.
Glad not to be a stray.

Trudy L. Himes

I
saw
a stray
along
my way,

All
fur
and bones
and
tail.

He looked
at me
with
eyes of
gold

and
followed
while
he
wailed!

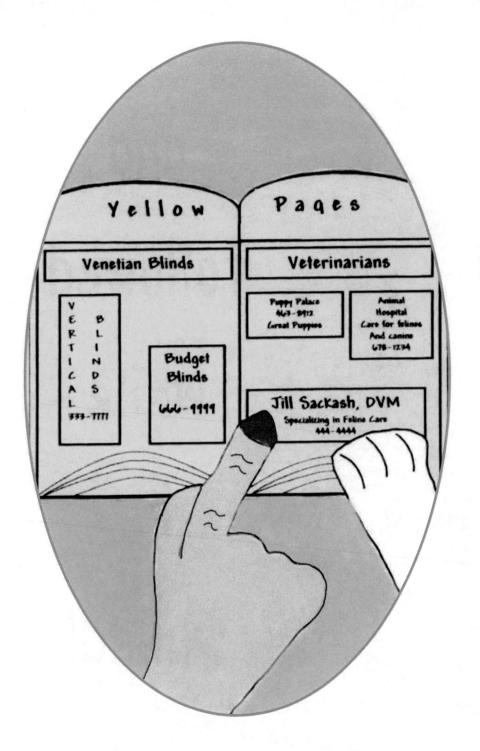

Home
we went
to find
a
Vet,

He
looked
so ill
and
frail.

A
pill or two
and
lots of
Love

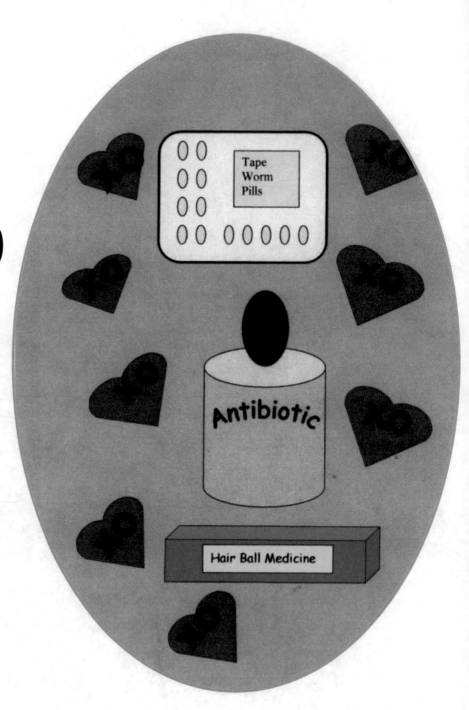

Now
finds
a
wagging
tail!

He

wears

a coat of

Gray and

White,

A
tailor
made
tuxedo!

Not
always
needing
formal
wear,

He
travels
incognito!

His
normal
bath
does not
suffice.

He

showers

with

me

daily!

Now's the time he gives advice

And
sings
like
Pearl Bailey!

Looking

fit

for

basketball,

His
shape
betrays
his
vice.

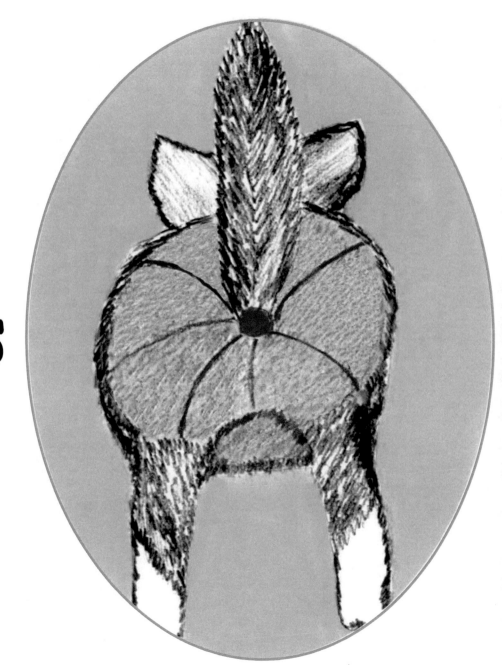

Having

snacks

beneath

the

sun,

Mouse Trap Menu

Mousetizers
Jumbo Mouse Cocktail
Mouse on the half shell
French Mouse Soup

Salads
Mouse Trap House Salad
Smoked Mouse with Catnip Salad
Caesar Mouse Salad

Entrees
Big Mouse Burger
Bar-B-Qued Mouse
Deep Fried Mouse
Mouse Burrito
Mousey Cristo Sandwich

All entrees served with Fried Mouse
Tails and a Catnip Salad

Desserts
Mouse Mousse
Mouse Brule'
Mouse Strudel Pie

Look out

you

fat

sweet

mice!

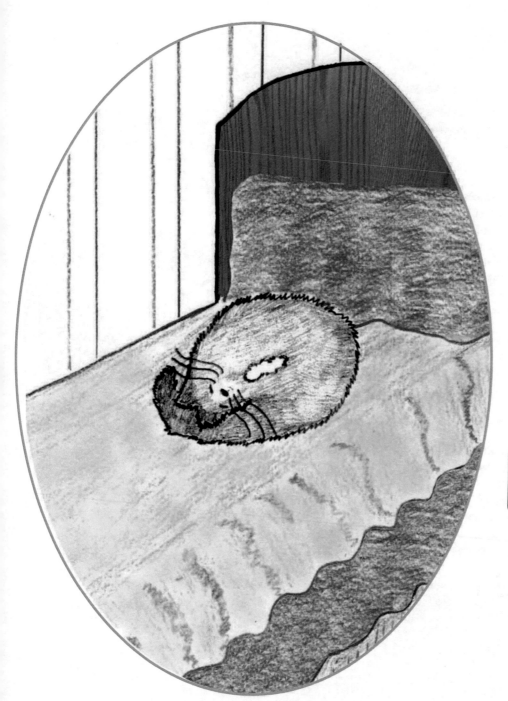

On
my bed
he
loves to
sleep,

For
hours
he's
curled
away.

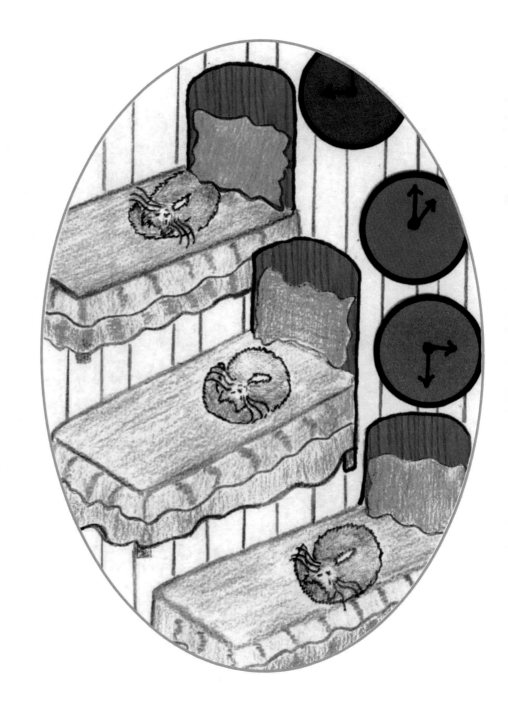

Throughout the night he purrs his thanks,

Glad
not
to be
a stray!

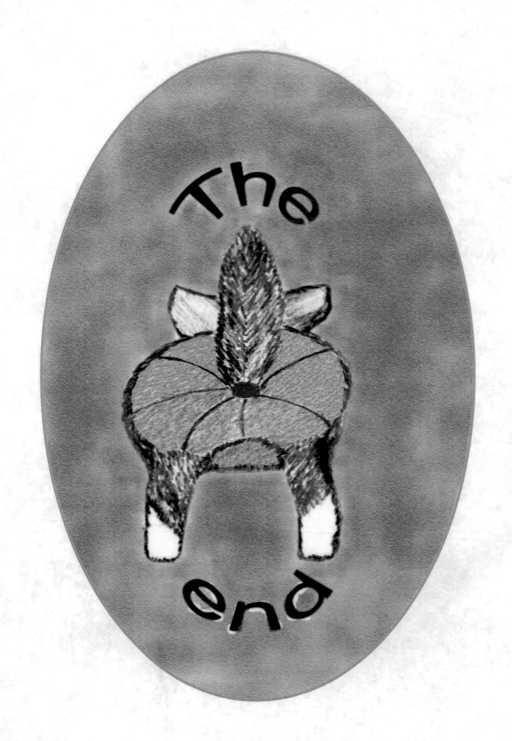